Contents

'Gardener' Henry VIII practising his topiary skills, as depicted in these details from a London Transport poster of 1922.

Welcome to Hampton Court Gardens

Close by those Meads for ever crown'd with Flow'rs
Where Thames with Pride surveys his rising Tow'rs

'Hampton Court Gardens have atmosphere in spades.'

For gardener, writer and presenter Alan Titchmarsh it is the Privy Garden (pictured) that is the jewel in the crown.

When I first visited Hampton Court, around 35 years ago, I remember that particular stretch of the grounds being nothing more than an overgrown Victorian shrubbery – a mixture of dark-leaved evergreens that looked forbidding in all weathers. To sweep them away took courage and a fair old investment, but the gamble paid off and the palace now has a William and Mary garden that is worth travelling miles to see.

Watch it at different times of day. You'll see those spiky yew sentinels acting like gnomons on a giant sundial. The pattern of shadows changes with the hours and so does the garden's character. Walk down the central axis towards the fountain, and then turn back and look at the palace, now perfectly set off by the crisp formal planting. Walk further until you reach those remarkable Tijou gates, and see how their gilding sparkles in the sun.

The Privy Garden is all about grandeur and opulence, rather like the palace itself, and from time to time we all need a bit of grandeur and opulence in our lives.

You can fill an entire day at Hampton Court without ever going inside the palace. You can marvel at the sparkling canal that is King Charles II's Long Water – dug out on his return from exile in France to demonstrate to those who mattered that the Crown was back and with it the king's power, not to mention his refined taste in gardens – a taste developed on the Continent.

From Henry VIII to Elizabeth I, from Charles II to William and Mary, the Georges, Victoria and Elizabeth II, the gardens here resound with echoes of our history. There may be little or nothing of Henry VIII's garden in evidence now (for children have always swept away their parents' ideas and replaced them with their own), but what Hampton Court does have in spades is the atmosphere created by this rich history.

I have been to many gardens in Europe – from Versailles in France, to the Boboli Gardens in Italy and the Summer Palace in Russia, and I can honestly say that none of them has the atmosphere and spirit of the gardens at Hampton Court. I hope you come away being as passionate about them as I am.

A potted history

My garden sweete, enclosed with walles strong, Embanked with benches to sytt and take my rest; The knots so enknotted, it cannot be exprest; With arbours and alyes so pleasant and so dulce The pestilent ayers with flavours to repulse.

Cardinal Wolsey's gentleman usher, George Cavendish, *c*1527

The gardens at Hampton Court Palace were, for their first 200 years, the playground of the kings and queens of England. Here, they might watch their flowers grow, dally with a new romance, compete in sporting activity or mull over their worries. These concerns became part of the history of the land, from Henry VIII's courtship of Anne Boleyn to the angry scenes between Frederick, Prince of Wales and his father, George II, the last king to stay at the palace.

New ideas and plans for gardens arrived with each successive reign, from the early 16th century, when Cardinal Wolsey laid out the first small knot garden, through the late 17th century's fine baroque gardens, including the ever popular maze, to today's annual Flower Show, where contemporary garden schemes compete for awards for excellence. Throughout its history, Hampton Court Palace has been at the cutting edge of garden design.

The famous gardens of Hampton Court in 1712, as seen in this bird's-eye view from the east, by Leonard Knyff, *c*1712 and (inset) earlier from the south, sketched by Knyff *c*1702.

A list of palace gardeners and designers between 1660 and 1760 reads like a *Who's Who* of gardening history:

Adrian May,
John Rose,
André and Gabriel Mollet,
Daniel Marot,
George London,
Henry Wise,
Lancelot Capability Brown.

The area around the palace has served several functions. The waterside provided a pleasant view from the raised Tudor banqueting house, but it also ensured fast river transport for both king and provisions. When, eventually, the royal barge no longer made its sedate progress along the Thames to Hampton Court, pleasure boats brought day trippers from the poorer areas of London, delighted to be exchanging 'the contagion of the town' for the quiet good air of the palace gardens, one of the first out-of-town attractions to be opened on a Sunday for the rising number of the working population with weekend leisure hours.

Fallow deer in Bushy Park.

Hunting, shooting and fishing

In the 16th century, the estate encompassed vast tracts of land in Surrey and Middlesex and was a royal hunting park. **Henry VIII**, who loved the thrill of the chase, revived the concept of the medieval deer park, reserved for the exclusive use of the king. Today, Bushy Park, to the north of the palace, retains its herds of red and fallow deer. The Home Park, adjoining the gardens of Hampton Court, is still home to fallow deer and a host of wildlife that includes several endangered species as well as some new arrivals.

For over a century now, hunting has given way to golf. The palace gardens themselves have always found a place for the gentler royal sports. Besides a tiltyard, Henry VIII had bowling alleys, archery grounds and tennis courts. Real tennis continues to feature as an important palace activity.

Areas of the garden were set aside to grow food for the vast numbers of the court who accompanied the sovereign to the palace. In the 16th century there were already freshwater fish ponds known as 'stewponds', fruit orchards and beehives, as well as vegetable and herb gardens.

At the end of **William III's** reign Hampton Court had one of the largest and most impressive kitchen gardens in England, and was renowned for its variety of fruit trees.

Choice fruit for the royal table continued to be grown until the early 19th century, when the kitchen gardens made way for flower gardens developed for public enjoyment. Old varieties of espaliered fruit trees have recently been replanted in parts of the former kitchen gardens near the Clore Learning Centre, while in the nurseries, palace gardeners lovingly tend the regenerated historic royal collection of exotics, besides growing half a million bedding plants a year.

Historically, all these uses, however, were ancillary to the principal theme: the pleasure garden - an imposing showpiece, reflecting the power and status of its royal owner. In the hands of a master gardener, exotic plants, garden architecture and exquisite sculpture were all combined into a harmonious and regal spectacle of magnificence.

Royal gardeners

Henry VIII soon stamped his ownership firmly on Wolsey's garden, transforming it into an ostentatious heraldic garden where carved and gilded animal sculptures displayed royal coats of arms. Echoes of this style can still be seen in the stone beasts at the entrance to the West Front and the heraldic figures with glittering pennants on the roof of the Great Tudor Hall.

Queen Elizabeth I was to develop knot gardens further until they formed an embroidery of flowers,

of the kind seen in paintings of rich Elizabethan costumes. It was during her reign that many flowers familiar to us today, such as sunflowers, African marigolds and larkspur, were introduced, adding vibrant colour.

Queen Elizabeth I, standing in front of a walled garden, in a painting by Marcus Gheeraerts the elder, c1580-85.

By the 17th century the knot garden was considered old fashioned and **Charles I** introduced a simpler Italianate style of garden, featuring grass or gravel areas or 'plats', each showcasing a central piece of statuary. After the king's execution, the privy garden was developed by the palace's new resident, Oliver Cromwell, who brought some of the late king's classical sculpture to Hampton Court.

At the restoration of the monarchy in 1660 **Charles II,** influenced by years of continental exile, initiated the Long Water and its double avenue of lime trees. This was an introduction to the French formal garden, which its greatest pioneer, André Le Nôtre, was on the point of bringing to full flower for Louis XIV at Versailles.

Above: Charles I, who introduced the Italianate style, with his consort Henrietta Maria, by Daniel Mytens, c1630-32.

Left: Statue of Bacchus that now stands in the Privy Garden, re-carved by Neil Simmons, after the original 17th-century figure.

A young William of Orange (later William III) with garlands of flowers and fruit by Jan Davidsz de Heem, 1672.

But it was **William III** from the Netherlands and his queen, **Mary II**, who left the most lasting impression on the gardens at Hampton Court. It was their craftsmen who synthesised the elements, creating a romantic harmony between Wren's new palace and the baroque garden, which remains its underlying structure today.

The Huguenot Daniel Marot designed not only the Great Fountain Garden, but also delftware and fabrics to furnish the royal interiors. Master blacksmith Jean Tijou created the boundary screens and railings for the gardens as well as all the staircases within the new palace. Sculptor John Nost made lead figures for the garden and for Wren's building. The potters at Delft created magnificent blue and white flower pots for Queen Mary's gardens and for her gallery.

Flowers inside the palace; detail from the north wall of the King's Staircase.

Queen Mary's favourite pots have been reproduced for the Lower Orangery Garden.

The artist Antonio Verrio, who had also been master gardener to Charles II and James II, painted the flowers blooming in William's gardens onto the ceilings of the King's Bedchamber, entrance staircase and Banqueting House. Grinling Gibbons carved them in limewood; echoing the avenues of newly planted trees.

George II's consort, **Queen Caroline**, and later Lancelot Brown, were both extremely influential in the formation of the 18th-century English landscape garden, so it is surprising that the old fashioned formal gardens of Hampton Court survived. By the time Capability Brown came to Hampton Court, royalty had stopped coming, and there was finance only for basic garden maintenance. Brown simply ceased to prune the topiary, resulting in the huge yew trees, now so characteristic of Hampton Court, that were re-shaped from the early 20th century.

19th-century visitors enjoying the Broad Walk, painted in watercolour by Thomas Robert Macquoid, c1860.

Pleasure gardens

With the opening of the palace gardens in the early 19th century, new mass bedding displays and herbaceous borders were created for the visiting public.

Yet alongside the new there were nostalgic attempts to re-create the lost historic gardens. One such is Ernest Law's early 20th-century knot garden on the south side of the palace. Modern technology has aided restorations of the Privy and Lower Orangery Gardens, and the recent replanting of the Long Water Avenue is firmly underpinned by documentary and archaeological investigation.

Today the estate, while absorbing major functions and events such as the annual International Music Festival and Flower Show, maintains a delicate balance of conservation, care, maintenance, restoration and re-creation for today's visiting public within the historic nature of the royal gardens of Hampton Court.

The tranquil Great Fountain Garden, looking towards the East Front.

The Tiltyard Gardens

A delightful spot in which to picnic or enjoy lunch in the café, this area includes the herbaceous and rose gardens, and has long been associated with the cultivation of fruit and vegetables for the royal table.

Royal tournaments were already outdated, a nostalgic lost dream of chivalry, by the time the 37-year-old Henry VIII decided to lay out a tiltyard to the north of Hampton Court Palace in 1537.

Regardless of the fact that it was unlikely to be much in use for jousting, Henry pursued this pageant of Tudor magnificence, creating five brick viewing towers for the ladies to dangle their favours from, although the only use recorded for the towers seems to have been as quarantine accommodation for a party of priests with the plague!

Henry's original Tiltyard towers are to the left of this view of Hampton Court Palace from the north by Wyngaerde, c1555.

Charles II found it a useful place to graze his horses, but William III saw more potential in this area and divided the land into six walled kitchen gardens – the grandest in England - in which to grow vegetables for the royal table. He also planted espaliered fruit trees, such as apples, peaches, plums and figs, which flourished against the shelter of the brick walls. Some of these espaliered fruits have recently been replanted around the Clore Learning Centre and on the walls of the herbaceous garden.

In the reign of George III, it became clear that royalty would not re-occupy the palace and the kitchen gardens were franchised to a succession of market gardeners, including Mr Jackson, a gardening greengrocer and nursery supplier from Kingston, who installed himself in the surviving Tudor tower and sold his choice produce, grown in the Tiltyard, from the palace gate.

Taking tea in the new tearoom in 1926.

From the 1920s, it was in the Tiltyard that the needs of the visiting public to the gardens at Hampton Court were addressed for the first time in a comprehensive manner. The surviving Tudor tower was converted into a tea room, and the surrounding areas adapted for gentle pastimes such as putting, bowling and tennis, with a pavilion in what is now the herbaceous quarter. Public lavatories were added, and a new requirement, car parking space.

These improvements resulted in a contentious entrance charge of one penny to visit the 'transformed' Tiltyard. Although the putting and bowls have long since disappeared, and the little-used tennis courts were removed quite recently, this robust area still houses many of the visitor services and is an ideal area in which to picnic.

Above: Elegant tennis players gather for 'Sunday Afternoon in the Tiltyard', drawn by A Forestier (Illustrated London News, 8th August 1925).

Right: A costumed interpreter walks his buckhounds, originally Tudor hunting dogs, through the garden.

The Herbaceous Garden

This is a tranquil midsummer delight, with its large luxuriant beds brimming over with old English flowering favourites, golden rod, phlox, asters and peonies. Outside the path on the opposite side to the pavilion has become known as Vrow Walk, possibly from the Dutch word vrouw, for lady, as it may have been a favourite promenade of the ladies of the family of George III's exiled Dutch cousin, to whom he gave apartments in the palace at the turn of the 19th century.

Rosa Centifolia (Cabbage Rose) by Pierre-Joseph Redoute, one of the earliest roses to be grown at the palace.

The Rose Garden

In the 1930s an informal rose garden was made in one of the walled compartments of the old kitchen gardens, rekindling a little of the lost romance of the Tiltyard, and evoking scented visions of romantic trysts and ladies in crinolines. Many of the old-fashioned English roses still bloom here in the form of new disease-resistant varieties.

Three statues were added to the garden in 1994, exiles from the Privy Garden restoration (see page 21). The two standing figures represent Adonis (or Summer) and Flora (or Spring). The woman with young children at the garden's centre is Abundance, carved in stone by Derwent Wood in 1947.

The sundial outside the Tiltyard restaurant was given to the palace in 1929 and once belonged to the great 18th-century actor, David Garrick. It stood in the garden of his villa, a stone's throw along the Thames.

13

A taste of the good life

The Kitchen Gardens at Hampton Court were, by the end of the 17th century, the most impressive in England. However creating your own kitchen garden – be it large and elaborate or simply a few attractive pots in a tiny back yard – is not difficult, explains writer, broadcaster and author, Pippa Greenwood.

There is something hugely satisfying about growing your own food, and despite the fact that we are now surrounded by places where we can buy perfectly good fruit, vegetables and herbs, there is nothing quite like freshly harvested, superbly tasty home grown crops.

The basics

Location: You need a sunny or only slightly shaded spot, sheltered from the worst of the weather and as large as you can manage. If space is short you can still grow an amazing amount in a plot only a couple of metres square. You will need to be strict with yourself about sowing or planting only a few of each crop you choose.

Soil: A moisture retentive soil that is full of nutrients will help healthy growth. If your soil is not quite up to scratch then incorporate garden compost or well-rotted manure.

Growing from seed: Most vegetable seeds are sown between January and July, details will be found on the seed packets. Take time to look through several different seed catalogues and select exactly what you want.

Containers

If you choose to use containers then it is best to get pots as large as possible as this will mean better results. The pot should be at least 30cm (12in) diameter, ideally 45cm (18in) and a similar depth, but the bigger the better. Most crops grow amazingly well in good-sized containers: try peppers, tomatoes, aubergines, dwarf runner beans, carrots, beetroot, lettuce, chard and even potatoes. All herbs thrive in pots, and you can also get a good crop from many fruits, especially strawberries.

'Ornamental kitchen gardening' is another way to save space, as you just incorporate your vegetables in with your ornamentals.

It may come as a surprise just how attractive many vegetables are. I love the look of courgettes clad with yellow flowers, wigwams of runner, or climbing beans, French beans, rows of rich red or tan brown onions, frilly-leaved green, or pinkish purple lettuces, brightly coloured stems of chard or those irresistibly beautiful leaves of radicchio.

And that is just the vegetables – herbs, and of course fruit trees and bushes, all have their own appeal, especially if you choose varieties with their appearance as well as taste in mind.

If you are new to all this, and perhaps feeling a little cautious, start with some of the easier edibles. Courgettes and marrows, beans (French, runner, dwarf, broad or borlotti-types for drying), tomatoes, potatoes, radish, lettuce, leeks and beetroot, and onions and garlic from sets are all easy.

Once you've been well and truly bitten by the bug, then venture out and try your hand at carrots, peppers, aubergines, brassicas, sweet corn or sweet potatoes. Even these are not that hard, and if time is short you can always buy in a few small plants to get yourself started. Give growing your own a go and you will never look back!

The Privy Garden

In 1533 Henry VIII was the first to create a private garden on the south side of the palace and the monarch's own garden has ever since been located between the king's apartments and the river.

Henry's garden was an ostentatious display of heraldic statuary and coats of arms; today's sculptured, calm space, restored in 1995, recreates William III's privy garden of 1701.

The Tudor garden was divided into 20 knot gardens, small squares each patterned with coloured sand and flowers such as sweet william, primrose, violet and strawberry plants. The squares were divided by a central path, bordered with rails and broken at intervals by green and white poles. On these stood 90 carved heraldic beasts, each holding high a gilded vane.

The terraced area of the palace was planted with a small orchard of damson, apple and pear trees. At the river end of the garden a mount was made, on which was built a banqueting house, its many windows providing panoramic views over the surrounding countryside. The spiral path up to it, described as having 'the turnings of cockle shells' was edged with rosemary, bay and cypress trees. At the base of the mount a triangular garden contained holly and pear trees, a fountain and possibly a hedge maze. Beyond, lay the great Watergate, the berth for the royal barge. This was a two-storey, brick building, with a large oriel window overhanging the river. Along the raised walk back to the palace on the east side were small towers giving views over the deer park.

Elizabeth I's French gardeners refined the knot gardens, introducing new heraldic patterns, with topiary cut into whimsical forms, and added two marble fountains, but the basic garden design remained unchanged. It was not until the advent of Charles I that a new privy garden emerged that was radically different.

The elegant scrolled design of the parterre.

The overcomplicated knot squares were swept away and replaced by a simple Italianate parterre of four grass plots, or 'plats', in the centre of which were to stand four statues: Adonis and Apollo in marble; Venus de Medici and Cleopatra in bronze. It was through this unfinished garden that, late one November afternoon in 1647, Charles I, prisoner in his own palace, made a bid for France and freedom. He escaped only to be recaptured and imprisoned at Carisbrooke on the Isle of Wight, before returning to face execution at Whitehall.

After the king's death, Oliver Cromwell, now Lord Protector, made his home at Hampton Court, bringing Charles I's fountain, Arethusa, from Somerset House as a central feature for what was now the regicide's Privy Garden.

One of the 12 panels of the screen made by Jean Tijou in 1702, which forms the southern boundary of the Privy Garden.

Opposite: The Privy Garden in spring.

With the arrival of William and Mary in 1689, Hampton Court acquired a greater importance than since the time of Henry VIII and both palace and gardens underwent a major transformation. While Christopher Wren was rebuilding the old Tudor palace, the Privy Garden became littered with the necessary building materials and stores. Undaunted, Mary made herself a temporary home in the Water Gallery, Henry VIII's old Watergate, which she turned into the 'pleasantest little place', furnishing it with blue and white Delft tiles, mirrors, paintings, flowers arranged in elegant Delft vases and commissioning Jean Tijou, the French master blacksmith, to construct a charming blue and gilt balcony to overlook the Thames.

Demolition of the old banqueting house allowed the statue of Arethusa to move to the river boundary, while a gazon coupé - an expanse of lawn with shapes of coloured sand cut into the turf - replaced the grass plats. Here, some of Queen Mary's exotic plants made their first English summer appearance.

The gentle, garden loving Queen Mary died from smallpox in 1694 and it was five years before William III contemplated new changes for the gardens at Hampton Court. His second privy garden - the restored garden you see today - was a parterre à l'anglaise, a garden in which the design is created in grass and outlined with borders of flowering shrubs and annuals. However, William was not to live to see its completion. He died in March 1702.

In the course of the 18th century, after Lancelot Capability Brown stopped pruning the topiary, the garden became so overgrown that eventually the small pyramid yews became 15m giants. The wonderful vistas were blocked and the relationship between the palace and the river, so dear to William III, was destroyed.

Following the refurbishment of the king's apartments after a serious fire at the palace in 1986, the decision was taken to restore William's lost garden. Copious documentation, plans and extensive archaeology provided all the information required and the restored garden was opened by The Prince of Wales in 1995.

This London Transport poster from 1927 by Dorothy Paton shows the figure of Adonis surrounded by towering greenery.

Above: The excavation revealed clearly the outline of the parterre of William's original privy garden, preserved beneath the topsoil.

Left: Visitors in the 1920s discovered a very different Privy Garden, with huge overgrown yew trees.

In spring, the borders of the parterre are filled with narcissi, tulips, hyacinths, iris and crocuses, while in summer marigolds, and other orange flowers for the House of Orange, feature prominently. A total of 3km of box give a fine edging. The huge oak frame of the bower is clad with hornbeam, not the wych elm of the original, which is susceptible to Dutch elm disease.

At the river boundary, Jean Tijou's masterpiece of wrought ironwork, commissioned by William III, has been partly regilded; restoration will continue for several years. The five Italian marble statues in the garden are copies of original figures which can now be seen in the Orangery.

Above: The restored garden looking magical after a light snowfall and **(left)** the newly planted garden in 1996.

Beauties and beasts

Statues add complexity to the natural beauty of the garden; sometimes placed to invite contemplation and sometimes to evoke awe. These are just part of the collection that you will encounter on your stroll around the gardens here at the palace.

Hero worship

Historically, statues were employed to display information about the identity of the estate's owner. Henry VIII did this in a very direct way, peppering his garden with carved heraldic beasts. William III, in a more subtle, but no less potent way, made use of classical figures to ascribe qualities to himself.

William's favourite subject was Hercules, the popular mythological Greek hero. This colossal lead figure of Hercules (left) stands with Mars, God of War, on the South Terrace (above). Both are ascribed to sculptor John Nost, c1691.

Stone roses

Sometimes statues invite reflection. In the Rose Garden, cold pale Adonis stares endlessly away from the lifeless marble form of Flora (right), the pair curiously divided by Abundance, surrounded in summer by a million scented colourful roses and in autumn by the poignant sight of a million faded blooms. Flora and Adonis were made in Carrara marble by Robert Jackson in 1869 and Abundance carved in English stone by Derwent Wood in 1946. All three figures stood in the Privy Garden before being moved here in 1993.

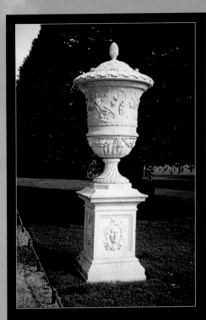

Size matters

Large urns and vases give gardens an air of gravitas and regal splendour.

The two great urns outside the palace on the east side stood originally in William and Mary's first privy garden. They were both carved in 1690 in Carrara marble, one with a theme of Bacchus (above), the god of wine, by Gabriel Cibber, and the other by Edward Pearce with a theme of water nymphs. When they were moved into the East Front Garden in 1701, two similar urns were commissioned to stand at the head of the Long Water. The carved pedestals on which these great urns stood can still be seen, but the urns themselves are in the Orangery at Kensington Palace.

Famous five

Apollo Gazing at the Sun (left) is one of the five marble statues now in the Privy Garden parterre, with Bacchus, god of wine, Ceres, goddess of the harvest, Vulcan, the gods' blacksmith, and Apollo and Marsyas. They were all recarved for the restoration of the Privy Garden. The 17th-century originals, shipped from Italy and offered to William III, are now too weather-damaged to stand outside and can be seen in the shelter of the Orangery.

Perfect blend

Sometimes sculpture sits so happily with its surroundings it can go unnoticed. The lead boys and flowerpots (below right) on the piers of the gate at the road end of the Broad Walk fall charmingly into this category, as does the enchanting little dolphin fountain (below top left) tucked away inside the wall of the Lower Orangery Garden. The flowerpots came from the workshop of John Nost c1700 and the dolphin fountain was made in Portland stone by Edward Pearce, c1691.

Censored!

Statues may evoke admiration of the human form... or sometimes not.

The bronze figures of Cleopatra and Venus de Medici, now in the Orangery, were purchased by Charles I and found their way to Hampton Court about the same time as Oliver Cromwell, prompting a scandalised Mrs Nethaway to write: 'one thing I desire of you - to demolish these monsters which are set up as ornaments in the Privy Garden'. The little lead Venus (below bottom left) who now shelters in her arbour at the end of the south sunken garden, next door to the Privy Garden, escaped there at the turn of the 20th century. Made by John Nost c1700, she was rescued from 'Mrs Grundy's Gallery', a large dark cupboard where the palace housekeeper kept any item she considered unfit for public exhibition.

The Pond Gardens

This protected, sunken area of the gardens has long provided an ideal place for exotic plants, particularly those collected by Queen Mary II, although it began life as a fish farm!

Above: This drawing of a medieval fishpond was adapted from a mural in the Pope's Palace in Avignon.
Below: A design made in 1903 by curator Ernest Law for the reinstatement of the Tudor ponds. This was never implemented.

At first glance, 'the Pond Gardens' is a curious name for a series of walled gardens, whose only relationship with water is three very small fountains. However, from Henry VIII's day and possibly before, this area of the garden had an important function, that of providing the resident court with fish for the many non-meat eating days of the pre-Reformation calendar.

The sunken areas were filled in 1535 by 'labourers ladyng of water out of ye Temmes to fyll the pondes', to form three ponds, one for breeding and the other two as holding ponds for fish ready to be netted and taken to the wet larder. The banks about the ponds were hedged with woodbine, whitethorn and hazel and inset into the still surviving walls were the Tudor green and white poles which held the king's heraldic beasts.

The recorded constant refilling of the ponds suggests that there were always leakage problems and by the end of the 17th century, the ponds had all but dried up.

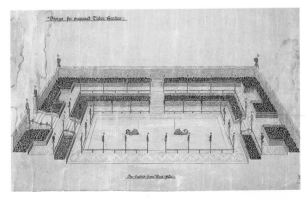

The sheltered gardens are always full of colour in spring.

It was to this ideally sheltered, sunken south facing part of the garden that Queen Mary brought the celebrated collection of exotics that she and William had amassed in the Netherlands, delivered by royal request from the furthest reaches of the newly discovered world by the enterprising Dutch East India Company.

Queen Mary used the first of the four walled areas adjoining the Privy Garden as a cut flower garden and retained some water in the form of two fountains.

In the next compartment she housed the important collection of orange and other citrus trees. This was not only fashionable, but a tangible iconographic statement for the head of the House of Orange. The citrus trees would have required protection indoors for the winter months (see page 30).

The third compartment was called the auricular quarter, where flowering bulbs, such as tulips and anemones, were grown alongside primulas or auriculas (literally, plants with ear-shaped leaves). The rarer or more flamboyant of these specimens were probably displayed in pots on tiered shelves. Flowers in season, particularly highly prized tulips, were arranged in the many magnificent blue and white Delft flower vases that Queen Mary commissioned and would have been brought into the palace or put into prominent locations in the gardens for royalty, courtiers and visiting guests to admire.

Right: This section of the Pond Garden was once Queen Mary's auricular quarter.

Mary II painted by William Wissing.

On the site of today's Lower Orangery Garden, three 'glass cases' stood in an area known as the greenhouse quarter. They were built in the Dutch style by the Dutch specialist Henrick Floris and gave the garden its new name: the Glass Case Garden.

They provided winter protection for the expanding collection of exotics, although in the summer months the plants would stand outside in pots.

In 1691 Queen Mary appointed the botanist Dr Leonard Plukenet at £200-a-year as superintendent to this important collection. The traveller Celia Fiennes, on a visit to Hampton Court in 1696, noted seeing: 'fine aloes, paricantha, myrtles, oranges and oliantas'.

At the end of the walk through the Pond Gardens is the Great Vine. This is of the Black Hamburg eating variety, planted in 1768 by Lancelot Capability Brown, making it both the largest and possibly the oldest vine in the world (see page 28). The vine keeper's cottage next door supports a venerable wisteria planted in the early 19th century.

On the site of Henry VIII's old riverside gallery, a new banqueting house was built for William III, with a painted interior by Antonio Verrio. To either side a terrace was made, affording views of the river through gilded iron grilles, now bricked in, set into the wall. They would also have given a view down on to the pheasant garden or aviary, known as the 'King's Aviary', where a variety of exotic birds such as linnets and goldfinches were housed in a semicircle of green-painted and gilded cages fanning out around a fountain.

An early 20th-century postcard of the Pond Gardens and the banqueting house.

In the early 20th century, the palace's curator and historian, Ernest Law, made plans to reintroduce the ponds into the Pond Garden. He failed in this enterprise but did manage to recapture a taste of Tudor times in the shape of an Elizabethan knot garden, laid out in 1924, which still occupies the plot under the windows of the Wolsey rooms, at the juncture of the Tudor and Baroque palaces.

A recently planted small orchard now occupies the late 17th-century flower garden. The adjacent sunken area, in which Queen Mary grew her orange trees, provides a sunny sheltered area in which flowering plants delight and thrive. Their brilliant spring and dazzling summer bedding displays, created by the palace gardeners, now make this one of the most popular and most photographed areas of the palace gardens.

Above: Ernest Law's Elizabethan knot garden.

Opposite: Imaginative and luxuriant bedding designs have created a colourful garden from Queen Mary's former orange quarter.

Grape expectations

A year in the life of the Great Vine – and the Vine Keeper.

Gillian Cox has tended and harvested the famous Hampton Court Great Vine – a Black Hamburg variety – for over 20 years. The sweet black dessert grapes are sold to visitors during September.

The Great Vine, which is the largest and possibly the oldest in the world, was planted in 1768 for King George III by Lancelot Capability Brown, the head gardener at Hampton Court Palace. Growing grapes in this expensive, labour-intensive fashion was a demonstration of wealth and status, as a vine keeper laboured year-round to provide exotic fruit for the royal table. Until 1920, the grapes grown here were for the royal family's exclusive consumption.

The new Vine House, with its public viewing cabin, was built in 1903.

Grapes being harvested and weighed in autumn 1924.

Gill's year:

October:

Both the vine and I have a well deserved break after the harvest. The vine sheds all its leaves, and I return refreshed, ready to start the clear-up operation.

November:

The vine is dormant enough to prune. I cut it back hard, taking off all the year's growth, right down to the larger branches, or rods.

January:

I embark on my least favourite and extremely dusty job – rubbing down the branches to remove the old bark that pests love to live in. Every few years at around this time the vine enjoys a good feed of well-rotted horse manure.

Feb/March:

Spring always comes early in the Vine House. I close the air vents, turn on the heating, water thoroughly and in the steamy atmosphere the vine begins to grow.

April:

The vine, which flowers briefly at the end of this month, is now at its most vigorous, growing at least 1cm a day! It produces far more shoots than can fit the space, so I spend the whole growing season controlling and training the vine to grow along the grid system.

Gillian assessing the crop before harvest. She tastes for sweetness, although in previous centuries eating the royal grapes was strictly forbidden and vine keepers numbered each bunch!

May:

The vine is still growing fast, but now the energy is going into making berries, which quickly form into bunches. I have to control the size of the crop by removing immature bunches to avoid either over-cropping, when one huge harvest means the vine will never fruit again. Although older vines can be erratic, I aim for a thousand bunches, which yield roughly 250 kilos of grapes.

June:

I protect the crop from mildew using mainly organic methods, although we spray with sulphur. The vine is a tough old thing, but the grapes are more vulnerable. One year a plague of wasps destroyed half the crop.

July:

The grapes now begin to darken to black, but they are not yet ready to eat.

August:

The grapes need about three weeks 'hanging black' to let the sugar develop in the fruit. I sample occasionally, of course!

September:

Harvest time! This means seven days-a-week of picking and selling for a whole month. I'm grateful for the help of volunteers. Every morning at 7.45am we start cutting down bunches, weighing and packaging, and they are on sale by lunchtime. You can't get much fresher than that!

Lower Orangery Garden

Once Queen Mary II's pride and joy, the Lower Orangery Garden evolved over the centuries into a commonplace expanse of lawn, until it was brought vividly back to life in 2007. The restoration project has created an authentic, unique replica of a 17th-century exotic garden.

The second or lower orangery was built by William III on the site of Queen Mary's original 'glass cases' in 1700, just six years after her death. It was here that the queen had grouped her collection of exotics.

These plants were spectacular at the turn of the 18th century, nothing like them had ever been seen before in Europe, and no effort or expense was spared to keep the tender plants thriving.

The range of plants that William and Mary brought to Hampton Court was vast, from cacti and succulents to tropical and sub-tropical specimens, collected as individual specimen plants, as much for their rarity as their beauty.

The collection boasted over 2,000 different species at its peak, many propagated from seed. Although today some may seem very commonplace, including aloe vera, now used widely in the cosmetic industry, there were pelargoniums, jasmine, agapanthus, pineapple and a collection of 1,000 citrus trees including Citrus Aurantium 'Bitter Orange', Citrus Sinensis 'Seville Orange' together with grapefruits and limes.

These exotic plants were over-wintered inside the Orangery, which today houses the Triumphs of Caesar paintings by Mantegna. In the summer months, the plants were brought out into the sunshine in costly and magnificent pots and stood in straight rows in front of the winter greenhouse. In the centuries following Queen Mary's death her collection was gradually dispersed until, by the 19th century, only a few orange trees could be traced back to the original collection.

It is this collection that has been lovingly re-formed by the gardeners at Hampton Court Palace over the past few decades: the original catalogue and manuscripts providing enough information for species to be gathered from the original sources.

In addition, contemporary accounts, engravings and garden plans enabled a picture to be formed of how the plants were set out in the summer months. This was further confirmed by archaeology that revealed long early 18th-century beds running parallel to the Orangery building. The beds have now been reinstated and planted with topiaried yews, cedars and junipers and round headed hollies with variegated box and Viburnum tinus. In between the formal planting, the exotics are set out in decorative pots (see panel).

Opposite: The summer display of exotics outside the Lower Orangery.
Inset: Reproduction terracotta flowerpot based on fragments found at William and Mary's palace at Het Loo in The Netherlands.

Replicas of the Delft pots so beloved of Queen Mary.

In the late 17th century, Queen Mary commissioned a variety of flowerpots from the finest pottery of the day, the Greek A Pottery at Delft in the Netherlands.

The blue and white pots in the newly-restored garden are replicas of such pots, made in the traditional way, using local clay and decorated with a tin glaze and skilled application of hand-painted decoration.

The smaller terracotta pots are copies of a royal flowerpot, reconstructed from fragments that were unearthed some years ago outside William and Mary's Dutch palace at Het Loo. The larger, glazed pots were copied from late 17th-century Dutch orange pots, which are seen in engravings of the period.

Moving orange trees in a 17th-century Dutch orangery.

The Great Fountain Garden

'The Gardens were noble and their Majesties' Designs yet nobler ...'

Stephen Switzer, 1682–1745

The colossal, toadstool-shaped yews of this garden have become indelibly associated with Hampton Court Palace. Some survive from the first garden on this site, but they were never intended to become this huge.

Charles II, returning to England in 1660, began the outline of a formal garden outside the East Front, on what was originally part of the larger hunting park. He had been inspired during his exile in the Netherlands and particularly France, where André le Nôtre had just relandscaped Vaux-le-Vicomte and was about to transform the gardens at the palace of Versailles.

This 1736 print shows elegant courtiers strolling in the gardens of the East Front.

André Mollet, Charles II's gardener and an expert in canal construction, cut a straight channel, edged with a double avenue of lime trees, out from the palace to the horizon. Its axis was the central gilded balcony fronting the apartments of the new queen, Catharine of Braganza. The couple honeymooned at Hampton Court, where they received a gift from the Venetian state of a gondola for the new canal, but the garden advanced no further.

A few decades later William III who 'found the air of Hampton Court agreed so well with him', had by 1689 devised a new scheme for the completion of Charles II's garden. He was accompanied by a team of talented gardeners and designers, including the French Huguenot, Daniel Marot. The palace end of the canal was filled in and on its site a great scrolled parterre, like a grand arabesque carpet, was laid out. It included 13 fountains, which gave the garden its

new name: the Great Fountain Garden. Four fine bronze statues were placed in the quarters of the parterre and four great marble urns installed, two at the head of the Long Water and two, which remain, outside the entrance to the palace. A gravelled Broad Walk, 20m wide, separated the palace from the garden; the wide herbaceous borders were late Georgian additions, created alongside the palace walls to the river and later in the opposite direction to the Flowerpot Gate on the Hampton Court Road.

The extensive iron railings and elaborate gates separating the gardens from the Home Park were made at this time by the French master blacksmith Jean Tijou. From either side of the Long Water two avenues of lime trees now also radiated from the palace, forming an extended goose foot or patte d'oie.

Daniel Marot's 1689 design for the Great Fountain Garden parterre.

Queen Anne simplified the parterre with 'new turfing and gravelling' and discarded the poorly functioning fountains, apart from the central fountain, which survives. To compensate for the lack of fountains, cross canals were added and the Tijou railings moved so that these canals were now enclosed in the gardens rather than in the park.

As the 18th century progressed, the formal garden lost favour with the sovereign so that Hampton Court was ripe for change. Its landscape could so easily have been transformed in the hands of Lancelot Capability Brown, who became its head gardener in 1764. However, Hampton Court was no longer the monarch's favourite palace, nor indeed now inhabited by royalty, and the only funding for gardens was for minimal maintenance. Out of respect for his profession, as he said, Brown left off pruning the topiary, and consequently giant shapes began to emerge in the East Front and Privy Gardens, as the yews and hollies grew finally to a long denied maturity.

From the opening of the palace gardens to the public in the early 19th century, the Great Fountain Garden became and has remained the focus of garden visits. Consequently it was in this garden that new planting schemes were introduced for visitors' enjoyment as it evolved into one of the first public parks and a model for many municipal English parks.

Massed bedding plants soon broke up the expanse of the former parterre, and the garden became famous for its annual spring and summer displays. From the early 20th century, the great yew trees surviving from the early scheme began to be pruned again, resulting in the present topiary giants.

At about the same time soft-coloured herbaceous border schemes were devised by Ernest Law, the palace's resident historian and curator. Recently, a large proportion of these have been reinstated.

The deep herbaceous borders on the Broad Walk recreate the original planting designs by Ernest Law in the early 20th century.

HAMPTON COURT

A Palace for Pleasures, Court Beauties, A Maze to get lost in, a Wilderness, Visitors welcomed in Kitchen and Wine-cellar.

BY TRAM FROM SHEPHERDS BUSH HAMMERSMITH or WIMBLEDON STN.

The inviting vista of the Great Fountain Garden in this London Transport poster of 1925 by Alfred Hayward.

The deep and dreamy borders inspired postcard artists too, as in this souvenir from summer 1913.

A grand day out

The appeal of the palace gardens has never wavered since they first opened their gates in November 1838. In the first year alone over 115,000 people arrived to see – and be seen in - 'London's Garden'.

The gardens were open from sunrise to sunset and entry was nominally free, (although the vine keeper called for a penny to see the Great Vine and the gardener demanded another penny for entrance to the maze), but these were merely side shows for the masses who came to enjoy what the newspapers now referred to as 'London's Garden'.

It was in fact one of the few attractions open on a Sunday, the only day working people had to visit. Visitors arrived by every possible means, from boat to charabanc (public coach), their journeys made easier by the rapid expansion of public transport – the railway reached Hampton Court in 1849. However, this sudden rush by Londoners to enjoy the delights of the palace gardens was not altogether welcomed by those who had previously enjoyed the exclusive right to them. The 'high in birth and low in pocket' grace-and-favour residents of the palace 'suffered dreadfully – particularly on Sundays, when they had for some time expected the earth to open and swallow the public up; but which desirable event had not yet occurred, in consequence of some laxity in the arrangements of the Universe'.

An attempt to remedy this 'laxity' was made by the Rev. D. Wilson, who described Sunday in Hampton Court gardens as 'hell upon earth; the people come intoxicated and the scenes in these gardens on the Lord's day are beyond description'. These complaints were countered by the palace chaplain who commented: 'The conduct of the masses is orderly, quiet and respectable, nor do I ever remember seeing a drunken character.'

The exact truth of the situation almost certainly lay somewhere in between. As the residents continued to complain of nude bathing, crying babies or men smoking near their open windows, so the number of visitors rose steadily, year on year. The palace residents retreated, cultivating idiosyncratic gardens in the corners of private courtyards or in areas of the Privy Garden, which remained closed to the public until the 1890s.

Meanwhile the public were eager for novelty and applauded the gardeners' attempts to put the palace gardens in the forefront of fashion. Carpet or mass bedding was pioneered with a patriotic display for the coronation of George V in 1911 and special Bluebell, Daffodil and Crocus Sundays were advertised. A regular spring visitor was his consort, Queen Mary. Today, over half a million visitors from all over the world come to these famous gardens, where there is always something new to be discovered.

'Every Saturday afternoon during the fine weather, a band of the cavalry regiment quartered at Hampton Court and Hounslow plays for two or three hours opposite the great east front of the palace, at which time the gardens receive most of the aristocratic visitors to Hampton Court.

Saturday is the fashionable day par excellence and the groups of well-dressed ladies seen in various parts of the grounds surrounded by the choicest productions of Flora, furnish pictures worthy of Breughell.'

Gentleman's Magazine, 1847

Fun for all: (from top:) paddle steamer *Queen Elizabeth* delivers tourists in 1911; well-behaved children pose in front of the Long Water; a 'launch load of lovely ladies' arrive in 1926.

Left: An early view of visitors seeing and being seen in 'London's Garden' by George Hilditch, *c*1849.

The Wilderness

'Nothing of that kind can be more beautiful than Hampton Court Wilderness,' observed Daniel Defoe. Today's Wilderness still evokes a delighted response from its many visitors.

This area of the gardens today is an attractive semi-wild area of flowering bulbs in the spring, and wild grasses, flowering shrubs and trees during the summer months. However, it was formerly a very different kind of garden. Wilderness derives not from 'wild' but from the German verb wilder which means to wander.

There was an orchard here in Tudor times – an assortment of ornamental and fruit trees set in long grass dotted with flowers; by chance, not dissimilar to what has developed here today. Two small bowers or banqueting houses provided a place in which to rest or take refreshment. On the side nearest the palace the orchard was bordered by a section of the former moat.

The origins of the formal gardens in this area are obscure. They may have been planned as private gardens to walk in by Lady Castlemaine, the imperious mistress of Charles II. In all events, by the end of William III's reign, a geometric pattern of small gardens had been laid out, surrounded by trim hornbeam hedges. Sanded or gravelled paths were walkways for daily exercise for the court and the quiet gardens gave a breath of seclusion close to nature.

In the interior of some of the compartments formed by the hedges shady elm trees were planted, providing little areas of seclusion and surprises (and possibly romantic trysts!). In others there were flowering shrubs, and two at least contained a maze. One, originally set out in hornbeam hedging, but now replanted in yew, is the maze that survives today (see page 40).

The Wilderness features in the early spring festival – Crocus Time – advertised by London Transport in 1935.

The other was described as Troy town maze, an ancient puzzle made from espaliers or cut turf whose form claimed to be derived from the Siege of Troy. The compartment gardens of the Wilderness gradually disappeared as the hedges deteriorated and were removed and the paths became overgrown and eventually lost.

The huge pine tree that marked the centre of the Wilderness has long since been cut down and flowering shrubs and trees have replaced the elms, decimated by Dutch elm disease in the 1970s. A rocky dell now marks the site of the Troy town maze.

Very much a 1960s addition, a laburnum grove makes an annual splash of bright yellow, but it pales into drabness compared with the real stars of the Wilderness, the flowering spring bulbs that spread over the entire grassed area as far as the maze, a dazzling carpet of purple crocuses and yellow daffodils and narcissi.

The central feature of the original Wilderness garden was a large pine tree seen here in John Spyers's painting *The Middle of the Wilderness Garden at Hampton Court*, c1780.

Lost in delight

No visit to the gardens is complete without a turn around 'The most famous maze in the history of the world' says Chief Curator Lucy Worsley.

The evidence for the original planting of the maze is quite appropriately lost in mystery. Some historians say it was planted by William III at the end of the 17th century, others think the payments for 'making a figure hedge Work of very large Evergreen plants in the Wilderness' that appear in Queen Anne's accounts mark its beginning. Everyone agrees, however, that the maze is the only remaining fragment of the much larger, lost Wilderness Garden.

Guidebooks to the palace reveal changing opinions on the maze: in 1724 Daniel Defoe thought of the whole Wilderness that 'nothing of that kind can be more beautiful', but by 1742, garden mazes had fallen out of fashion, and his words were rewritten: now, 'nothing can be more disagreeable than to be immured between Hedges'.

But when the palace was thrown open to the public from 1838 the maze quickly re-established itself as one of the most popular parts of a day at Hampton Court. In 1850 we hear that 'Many hours are spent by young persons, aye, and by the old too, in trying to discover the intricacies of the labyrinth'.

When Jerome K. Jerome, author of *Three Men in a Boat*, described a visit to the maze in 1889, his hero Harris fatally underestimated the difficulty of solving the puzzle. 'We'll just go in here, so that you can say you've been, but it's very simple,' he told his friends. 'It's absurd to call it a maze... We'll just walk around for ten minutes, and then go and get some lunch.' Needless to say, Harris and his friends got totally lost, and 'had to wait for one of the old keepers to come back from his dinner before they could get out'.

These 'old keepers' probably included the celebrated William Dodson. In 1898, at the age of 74, he was still collecting a penny per person after more than 40 years in the job.

Today the maze is as popular as ever all year round. Historic Royal Palaces' gardeners are gradually replanting the central portion of the maze with the original hornbeam. As you walk through the hedges you'll hear some intriguing sounds which are part of a sound sculpture installed in 2005 by the artists Greyworld.

Top right: Visitors getting happily lost at the turn of the 20th century.

Right: This postcard puzzle from 1832 gives a guide to kings and queens of England – but does it help you to the centre?

Opposite: Children getting 'thoroughly lost at a moderate cost' and not really enjoying it, in this whimsical London Transport poster from 1956.

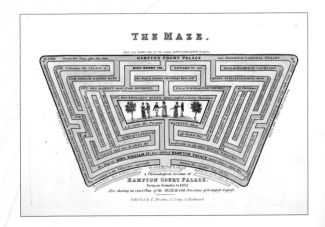

A harassed school teacher from Hayes
Took her children to Hampton Court Maze,
They got thoroughly lost
At a moderate cost
And then had a wonderful time admiring
the Great Vine and imagining Henry VIII
serving double faults on the Tennis Court.
It was easy to get there, too — Green Line
Coaches 716, 716A, 718 and 725 run to the gates.

Home Park

The Home Park provides the perfect setting for the formal gardens of Hampton Court, and a safe home for many endangered species of wildlife.

On one hand, walking through Home Park brings to mind the old hunting park, with rough grass and aged trees. An ancient oak, aptly nicknamed 'the Methuselah' could even be the last of the acorns planted by Harry Myles and John Gadsbe of Kingston in 1537. On the other hand, the canal, its flanking lime tree avenue and two diagonal avenues radiating for a distance of over 1 km from the semi-circle of the Great Fountain Garden, make the park an integral part of the famous late 17th-century baroque goose-foot layout. Seen from the air, this design is instantly and unmistakably recognisable as the giant footprint of Hampton Court Palace.

In his younger days, Henry VIII had enclosed vast areas of parkland around Hampton Court for hunting, but as he got older and fatter from the late 1530s, his hunting activities were restricted to watching deer coursing from his viewing towers in the walled-off chase of the Home Park.

Over 180 years later, Queen Anne, herself a keen hunter, similarly confined, evolved a different solution to her desire for hunting. She had riding paths created throughout the park for her one horse chaise, which she drove herself, even taking part in the hunt in this fashion.

When the formal gardens at Hampton Court were opened to the public in 1838 the gates of the Home Park remained firmly locked and it was only after repeated lobbying that the park was eventually partly opened to the public in 1893. A small herd of fallow deer were reintroduced at this time, and there was grazing for sheep and cattle.

Top: Home Park beckons beyond Tijou's elegant 17th-century railings.
Left: A swan on Long Water.
Opposite: Fallow deer graze in the wintry park.

Although the park was always prone to flooding, after its opening it soon became used for a variety of activities. In 1895 an 18-hole golf course, designed by Willy Park, who worked on Sunningdale, was laid out in the eastern corner and the Home Park Golf Club, which is still flourishing, was formed. Two years later the Hampton Court Model Yacht Club established a base alongside the Rick Pond where the miniature yachts still set sail. In the face of some opposition, rugby football pitches were installed for the local youths, who also enjoyed skating on the Long Water whenever the surface froze.

William III had kept a stud in Home Park, and this was updated and expanded in the early 19th century by George IV, who had a passionate interest in horse racing. After the Royal Stud moved to Sandringham in 1894, only one of the paddocks was retained. From the redundant paddocks land, allotments were created for the grace-and-favour residents of the palace, while the remaining portion became the 'Apprentices' Garden', an area set aside for teaching apprentice palace garderners. This area, now a secluded enclave, contains an interesting mini-arboretum and has been renamed the 20th Century Garden.

Over 500 trees were lost from the Home Park in the great storm of 1987. A period of restoration has followed, including the replanting of some of the historic avenues. Between 1990 and 1996 the cross avenues were replanted, and since 1987 over 2,000 new lime trees have been planted on either side of the Long Water. In due course the Kingston Avenue, centred on Kingston parish church tower and the Ditton Avenue which points toward Thames Ditton, will be similarly replanted.

Jubilee Fountain installed in celebration of the 50th anniversary of Queen Elizabeth II's accession.

The oldest surviving building in the Home Park is the ice house built by William III. The park's newest feature is the Jubilee Fountain at the end of the Long Water, which was put in to celebrate Queen Elizabeth II's Golden Jubilee in 2002. It consists aptly of five jets, the central one of which shoots a spout of water over 30m into the air at 15-minute intervals.

Above: Heron with snack, Long Water.

Opposite: Mistletoe seems to thrive at Hampton Court and it can be seen in great ornamental pompoms on many of the more mature trees, both in Home Park and within the palace grounds.

Park life

As the area around has become a densely populated suburb, so wildlife has looked to Home Park as a refuge.

The park has a rich ecology, and is listed as part of the London Borough of Richmond upon Thames Biodiversity scheme. It shelters a variety of birds from common rooks and robins, to the less often seen tawny owl and green woodpecker to the rarely seen skylark and kingfisher (right).

The Long Water hosts a variety of water fowl including Canada geese, coots and swans while a lone heron or cormorant can often be seen like a statue at the water's edge. Several varieties of bat have homes in the park and many of the dwindling numbers of stag beetles find shelter here. Some very noisy newcomers are the rose-necked parakeets that have colonised most of the area's local parks.

Rose-necked parakeet.

Sports of kings

Cardinal Wolsey's idyll of a quiet garden 'with benches to sytt' was rudely disturbed by the arrival of Henry VIII whose idea of a garden was an exciting place in which to exercise.

The king shot at painted butts or targets with an arquebus or hakbut (an early type of gun) in Wolsey's orchards and used the park for archery practice, in which he excelled, shooting 'as stronge and as greate a lengthe as anie of his garde'.

This was merely a warm-up for the principal sport of kings – hunting. Henry greatly extended his hunting park, taking delight in stag hunting, although in his later years his sport was restricted to deer coursing. This took place in a walled off area of the park where he watched from raised viewing points in the gardens.

Dogs were used for hunting and ferrets for chasing the black coneys or rabbits that had been bred on the estate since the Knights Hospitallers' occupancy. These were prized for their black fur, which only noblemen were entitled to wear. Pheasants were reared for sport and there was fishing in the river and local ponds.

By the time the Tiltyard was completed in 1537 Henry VIII's jousting days were over and there is no evidence to suggest it was used during his reign. Hunting, however, continued throughout the centuries, moving mostly to the new neighbouring park at Richmond from the early 17th century.

> What sport shall we devise here in this garden, To drive away the heavy thoughts of care? Madam, we'll play at bowls.
>
> Shakespeare 'Richard II', c1601.

If hunting was the sport of kings, tennis is the game of kings. Henry VIII had both indoor and outdoor tennis courts at Hampton Court.

Once skaters used the frozen Long Water; now each Christmas a temporary rink is erected on the palace's West Front.

James, Duke of York (later James II) playing tennis.

The present tennis court on the east front of the palace was built by Charles I and upgraded by Charles II, both keen players. The Stuart court is still in use and at most times open for the public to watch a game in progress. It remains a royal sport, played by at least one member of the present British royal family.

Bowls has been a popular garden game since at least the 16th century. Henry VIII had an indoor bowling alley 'by the Teemsyde' and an open air alley in the orchard for the sport. However, its main attraction often lay in the heavy betting that accompanied it, so much so that the game was outlawed to servants and working men in 1541.

The Georgians, however, were still playing bowls at the riverside Pavilion Green and probably gambling as much as they did on tennis and cricket matches. By the 19th century rugby and football pitches had been made in the Home Park and there was winter skating on the frozen ponds. Many of these activities were reintroduced into the palace gardens in the 20th century and skating has recently been added as a Christmas entertainment.

This splendid hunting scene was woven as a bed cover between c1590 and 1620 and doubtless caused vivid dreams!

The gardens today

Following in the sometimes muddy footsteps of long-gone gardeners, today's skilled team of 46, aided by summer seasonal workers and enthusiastic volunteers, work tirelessly to keep these famous gardens looking their best as Head of Gardens and Estates, Terry Gough, explains.

Restoring areas to their former glory is also an important part of their roles.

'Our youngest gardener is 25 and the eldest member of our team 63. Some gardeners have been working here for over 45 years, and know some of the mature shrubs and trees like old friends.'

We are all very proud of what we achieve at Hampton Court. In addition to the ongoing challenge of keeping these gardens looking gorgeous, we combine seasonal maintenance with major landscape conservation projects, such as the Privy Garden Restoration project in 1995 and the Lower Orangery Garden (see page 30).

Growing our own

All the work undertaken within the palace gardens and estate is mainly carried out by our own trained gardeners, with the exception of tree surgery and estate carpentry.

In the best traditions of the past, when garden apprentices learned their trade at the palace, our staff undergo regular training, both through regular practical workshops and though the opportunity to gain formal vocational qualifications. This enables us to retain a very highly skilled workforce, of which we are very proud.

The Glasshouse Nursery

The Glasshouse Nursery has a history going back over 300 years. During the reign of William III and Mary II it was known as the Melon Ground as it contained many 'hot' beds of heat-generating manure and tanner's bark that enabled gardeners to raise exotic seeds from all over the world under glass.

Today the Glasshouse Nursery team is responsible for growing 140,000 bedding plants and exotic plants each year. These include spring flowering plants such as violas, polyanthus, wallflowers and daisies, through to summer flowering plants such as geraniums, begonias, coleus and cinerarias. The nursery also holds the National Collection of Heliotrope.

In addition to the 140,000 plants grown each year in our nursery the Gardens and Estate team also plant in the region of 200,000 bulbs within the flower beds and the grass areas of the Wilderness. This ensures that Hampton Court Palace maintains rich and vibrant flower bed displays from early April right up until the end of September each year.

The nursery is also the hub of our Gardens Conservation Department, as it enables us to provide our staff with training not only in gardens conservation and landscape techniques, but also in the growing and propagation of many hundreds of different varieties of plants.

The 20th Century Garden

This tranquil area at the far end of the canal was used from 1974 until 1992 as a fertile training ground – hence its former name 'The Apprentice Garden'.

Young men (the first female gardeners were appointed in 1950) practised newly learnt skills here, including how to plant and nurture a wide range of trees and shrubs.

Today there is no need for the garden to remain a dedicated training area, as our trainees are involved in a wide range of restoration projects throughout the gardens. The garden is a unique sanctuary for those who want to sit in beautiful surroundings and enjoy the peace and tranquillity of bird song, away from the main visitor routes.

Showtime!

Two famous annual events provide an opportunity for the team to excel themselves: The Hampton Court Palace Flower Show and the Music Festival.

These provide the opportunity to delight many extra visitors, particularly the thousands of garden-lovers who visit the Flower Show and wander through the palace gardens at the height of their summer glory.

Of course, just like our colleagues who work in buildings and collections conservation, we share the challenge of mitigating the effect of thousands of visitors on the historic environment. It is our role to ensure the gardens are conserved not only for the immediate future, but also for future generations to enjoy what we have inherited, in some of the most famous gardens in the world.

The four seasons

A month-by-month guide to the gardens' must-see delights.

By **June** the rose garden is just coming into bloom and a wonderful fragrance fills the air for some distance around. In the evening the trees on the East Front are draped with lights for the picnickers attending the music festival, and a party atmosphere fills the gardens.

July in the Privy Garden sees the lavendula and honeysuckle in full flower; the lavendula brings an amazing purple flush to the whole garden. Home Park is full of life and colour, as thousands visit the annual RHS Flower Show.

The Great Vine is in full glory in **August**, bearing juicy bunches of Black Hamburg grapes ready for picking. All the summer bedding displays throughout the East Front, Privy and Pond Gardens are at their most spectacular.

'The summer's flower is to the summer sweet'

Shakespeare, Sonnet 94

In **March** the Wilderness becomes a creamy sea of yellow and white narcissus. Look out for the first flowering shrubs such as photinia and forsythia against the walls and in beds. On the East Front, don't miss the colourful crocus banks straight ahead of the Governor's Gate. The scent of the hyacinths fills the air.

The Pond, Privy and Lower Orangery Gardens' spring bedding displays are at their best in **April** and there's masses of colour in the East Front with the displays of tulip, narcissus, polyanthus and wallflowers. Enjoy the fleeting but gorgeous cherry blossom in the Wilderness.

The wisteria in **May**, in the Pond Garden and on the adjacent vine wall, are remarkable for both scent and tumbling colour. The milder weather sees the reappearance of the citrus, and exotics are brought out and displayed in their lovely ornate blue and white pots in the Lower Orangery Garden.

'I dreamed that, as I wandered by the way, 'Bare Winter suddenly was changed to Spring…'

Shelley 'The Question' 1822

Romantics will delight at the abundance of mistletoe in **December**: its distinctive balled clusters can be seen on the robinia tree on the West Front and also among the lime trees on the Long Water. In the 20th Century Garden a fine collection of holly trees add Christmas cheer.

Visit early in the day with your camera in **January**. In a hard frost the sculptural shapes of the evergreens in the Privy Garden are magical. On the East Front, look out for our fine collection of visiting and native birds: Canadian and Egyptian geese, mallards, coots and moorhens.

The outline of the yew trees is especially beautiful during a **February** snowfall. Look through the railings into Home Park to see the descendants of Henry VIII's fallow deer. And can you spot the first snowdrops in the Wilderness, as the gardens awaken for another glorious year?

'Clouded with snow
Cold winds blow,
And shrill on leafless bough
The robin with its burning breast
Alone sings now.'
Walter de la Mare 'Winter'

Autumn crocuses are an unexpected bonus of **September** colour in the Wilderness. The virginia creeper to the left of the Governor's Gate is now in fabulous autumn colour.

The symmetry of Privy Garden design appears at its finest, as the topiary of the taxus, lex and box edging is completed in **October**. You'll see gardeners planting for next year's spring display on the East Front, with the golden leaves of the lime tree avenues providing a mellow backdrop.

By **November**, the tree bark in the Tiltyard Gardens and Wilderness looks wonderful, while the secluded 20th Century Garden is a mass of late autumn colour.

'There is a harmony in autumn, and a lustre in its sky'
Shelley 'Hymn to Intellectual Beauty' 1816

Four more palaces to explore; hundreds of stories to discover

Tower of London

Gaze up at the massive White Tower, tiptoe through a king's medieval bedchamber and marvel at the Crown Jewels. Meet the Yeoman Warders with bloody tales to tell; stand where famous heads rolled and prisoners wept ... then discover even more surprising stories about the Tower!

Banqueting House

Walk in the footsteps of a dazzling company of courtiers who once danced, drank and partied beneath Rubens magnificent painted ceiling. This revolutionary building was created for court entertainments, but is probably most famous for the execution of Charles I in 1649. Spare him a thought as you gaze up at this ravishing painting – one of his last sights on earth...

Kensington Palace

Marvel at the stunning collection of English court dress in this stylish palace, a unique archive of royal fashion from the 18th century to the present day – including several evening dresses worn by Diana, Princess of Wales. Explore the magnificent State Apartments and take tea in the Orangery designed for Queen Anne in 1704.

We offer an exciting programme of events and exhibitions throughout the year. For more information details on tickets and how to find us, please visit **www.hrp.org.uk**

Kew Palace and Queen Charlotte's Cottage

Step into this tiny doll's house of a palace and experience the joys and sorrows of King George III and his family through a radio play and displays of fascinating personal artefacts. Stroll to Queen Charlotte's Cottage, built in 1770, where the royal family enjoyed picnics and peace in a tranquil corner of Kew Gardens.

Open April to October. Entry to Kew Gardens is required to visit Kew Palace and Queen Charlotte's Cottage.

Support us

Historic Royal Palaces is the independent charity that looks after the Tower of London, Hampton Court Palace, the Banqueting House, Kensington Palace and Kew Palace. Our aim is to help everyone explore the story of how monarchs and people have shaped society in some of the greatest palaces ever built.

We receive no funding from the Government or the Crown so we depend on the support of our visitors, members, donors, volunteers and sponsors.

Can you help?

We hope you thoroughly enjoyed your visit to Hampton Court Palace Gardens and have discovered more about the conservation of this magnificent building and grounds. Our work goes on; funds will always be needed to protect and maintain Hampton Court. Your donation means this valuable work can continue.

Please call our Development Department on **0845 389 3003** for more information or email **development@hrp.org.uk**

Join us!

Joining Historic Royal Palaces is the perfect way to explore the stories inside five extraordinary places that helped define this nation's history. What's more, you'll save money and contribute to the important work of conserving the palaces at the same time.

Membership is amazing value; it gives you the freedom to visit the Tower of London, Hampton Court Palace, the Banqueting House, Kensington Palace and Kew Palace (from April to October) as often as you like.

It also means you don't have to queue – simply walk in to experience and understand what makes the palaces extraordinary. Other benefits include exclusive members-only events, behind-the-scenes tours and great discounts in our shops and online.

Make a present of the past

As you step through the doors of a royal palace you enter the realm of strategy, intrigue, ambition, romance, devotion and disaster. What more inspiring gift could there be than a Historic Royal Palaces membership for someone with a love of history and amazing buildings with their beautiful contents and gorgeous gardens?

Enquire about becoming a member of Historic Royal Palaces and find out more about the range of benefits by calling **0870 751 5174** or visiting us online at **www.hrp.org.uk/supportus**

Further reading

Explore Hampton Court Palace:
An Official Guide
Historic Royal Palaces, 2008

The Gardens and Parks at
Hampton Court Palace
Todd Longstaffe-Gowan
Frances Lincoln 2005

Hampton Court:
A Social and Architectural History
Simon Thurley
Yale University Press, 2003

Hampton Court Palace:
The Official Illustrated History
Lucy Worsley and David Souden
Merrell in association with
Historic Royal Palaces, 2005

For Children
Power Palace:
Tales from Hampton Court
Elizabeth Newbery
Historic Royal Palaces, 2006

Historic Royal
PALACES

Historic Royal Palaces is the
independent charity that looks
after the Tower of London,
Hampton Court Palace, the
Banqueting House, Kensington
Palace and Kew Palace. We help
everyone explore the story of
how monarchs and people have
shaped society, in some of the
greatest palaces ever built.

We receive no funding from the
Government or the Crown, so
we depend on the support of
our visitors, members, donors,
volunteers and sponsors.

Acknowledgements

Published by Historic Royal Palaces
Hampton Court Palace
Surrey
KT8 9AU

© Historic Royal Palaces 2008

ISBN 978-1-873993-08-8

Written by Susanne Groom, with Sarah Kilby (page 28) and
Terry Gough (page 48)

Edited by Sarah Kilby and Clare Murphy
Pictures sourced by Susan Mennell
Designed by www.rarecorporate.co.uk
Principal photography by Nick Guttridge, with special thanks to
Robin Forster, Jenni Phillips and Lee Prosser.

Print: City Digital Ltd

Picture credits

Abbreviations: b = bottom; c = centre; l = left; r = right; t = top

Front cover photograph by Nick Guttridge; Front flap:
© London's Transport Museum (details); Inside front flap: © Historic
Royal Palaces (illustration by Stephen Conlin); Contents page:
© London's Transport Museum (details).
Inside back cover: © Historic Royal Palaces

© Ashmolean Museum, Oxford: p. 10cl; C.J. Bond: p. 24c;
© Copyright of the British Museum: p. 6 (inset);© Copyright the
British Museum (Natural History), Botany Library: 13t; Crown
copyright: Historic Royal Palaces: 9cl, 18bl, 18br; Ian Franklin
collection: p.40 (background), 40b; © Historic Royal Palaces: pp. 2-
3, 4-5, 6-7 (background), 7t, 8bl, 9 (background), 9tr, 9cr, 9br, 10t, 11,
12-13, 13c, 16 (background), 16t, 16b, 17, 19 (background), 19t (William
Page), 19b, 20 (including background) 21, 22 (Vivian Russell), 22
(inset), 23 (including background), 24b, 25t, 25b (Vivian Russell),
26, 27cr, 27bl (Vivian Russell), 28tl, 28c, 28-29 (background), 29, 30
(main and inset), 31t, 32-33 , 34-35 (background), 34t, 35tr, 36-37,
37(inset), 37br, 38, 40t, 40c (Vivian Russell), 42, 43, 44, 45tl (Vivian
Russell), 48-49, 50-51, 51 (inset), 52t, 52b, 53t, 53b (Steve Bicknell,
Icarus Arts Publishing); © Historic Royal Palaces/newsteam.co.uk:
47tr; Les Strudwick collection: pp. 35br, 37tr, 37cr; © London's
Transport Museum: pp. 18t, 35bl, 39t, 41; Mary Evans Picture Library:
24t, 37(background); Mary Evans Picture Library/Illustrated London
News: p. 10b; Musée des Beaux-Arts de Lyon © MBA Lyon/Photo
Alain Basset: p. 9tl; Musée du Louvre, Paris/Giraudon/The
Bridgeman Art Library: pp. 14-15; Museum Boijmans Van Beuningen,
Rotterdam: p. 34b; Private Collection: p.8t; © Popperfoto/Getty
Images: p. 28cr; The Royal Collection © 2008, Her Majesty Queen
Elizabeth II: pp. 6-7, 8bl, 27tl, 47tl; © Royal Horticultural
Society/Lindley Library: 49 (background); The State Hermitage
Museum, St. Petersburg. Photograph © The State Hermitage
Museum (inventory no. 7650): 39b; Superstock: 45tr, 45bl, 45br;
© V & A Images/Victoria and Albert Museum, London: pp. 46-47;
© Wageningen Agricultural University, Netherlands: 31b.

Historic Royal Palaces is a registered charity
(no 1068852)

www.hrp.org.uk